# Building Credit for Your Business

Eagle Publications

Copyright 2013 Eagle Publications.

*Eagle Publications*
*Baltimore, Maryland*

All Rights Reserved

Distributed by Eagle Publications

No part of this publication may be copied in whole or part, without express written permission from the publisher.

10 9 8 7 6 5 4 3 2 1

# DISCLAIMER

Eagle Publications makes no claim as to the validity of the information contained within the booklets it sells and the vendors listed within those booklets. All information contained within the books and documents that we sell is provided "as is" with no guarantee as to its effectiveness. Eagle Publications hereby disclaims any and all responsibility for the manner in which the information contained within its documents is used by you. In no event will Eagle Publications be liable for any special, indirect or consequential damages or any damages whatsoever resulting from the loss of use, data or profits arising out of or in connection with the use or performance of information available within our documents. The documents and related listed vendors published within these documents may include technical inaccuracies or typographical errors.

Due to the nature of business, economical outlooks, etc., it is likely that the information provided herein can and will change periodically. To this end, the reader makes purchase of this product with the understanding that the information will likely be updated from time to time, rendering the book, in part, to be inaccurate until the updates have been made. The reader further understands that the updates will be made with no further notice to them that any information has changed. If the reader remains a member in good standing through our website, the updates will be made available to them at no further charge. If their membership to our website lapses, they must purchase the new version of the book in order to gain access to the changes.

If at any time, any of the information in this disclaimer becomes unacceptable to you, you should immediately stop using the product.

# CONTENTS

DISCLAIMER

INTRODUCTION

TRADE NAMES, TRADEMARKS & SERVICE MARKS

WHAT IS BUSINESS CREDIT?

WHY DO YOU NEED BUSINESS CREDIT?

WHEN SHOULD YOU BUILD BUSINESS CREDIT?

WILL BUSINESS CREDIT HELP YOU TO SECURE A BUSINESS LOAN?

THINGS TO AVOID WHEN BUILDING BUSINESS CREDIT

WHAT ARE BUSINESS CREDIT BUREAUS?

WHERE DO BUSINESS CREDIT BUREAUS GET THEIR INFO?

WHO ARE THE BUSINESS CREDIT BUREAUS?

HOW TO SETUP A NEW BUSINESS

ASSET PROTECTION

ABOUT BUSINESS STRUCTURES

COMPANIES THAT OFFER NET 30 TERMS

COMPANIES THAT OFFER REVOLVING CREDIT

OTHER RESOURCES

# INTRODUCTION

Obtaining business credit is no different from obtaining credit on a personal level. The thing is, if your personal credit is good, it's much easier to business credit. If your personal credit is bad however, it's more difficult to get business credit, but it's not impossible. As a matter of fact, in many cases, it may be **_EASIER_** to get business credit than it is on the personal level.

Each company that you encounter when trying to establish business credit, will have its own set of criteria and policies that they follow before they will grant you credit. Where possible, we have listed the general criteria along with the difficulty of obtaining credit with that company. Remember though, that the criteria the company follows may change from time to time, so the information given in this book may be inaccurate by the time you use it. The good news, is that anyone who buys our books and remains a member of our website, will have access to these changes as they become available.

One of the first things that you need to know is to SKIP services that help you to build your credit. First of all They are going to charge you high fees to do things that you should be doing yourself. The fact is, they are going to target the ones that they know are easy approvals. Second, while they may promise you business loans, the truth is, they will not be able to deliver that coveted part of business credit to you.

Building a credit file takes a great deal of time and effort, and frankly, in many cases, businesses that have a 5-year track record of good pay, *STILL* find it hard to be approved for business loans. In most cases, business loans involve close working relationships with the bank from which you are seeking funds. This history includes banking with the institution that you are trying to get the loan from. You'll learn more about that later however. In order to get your business established and start a credit file, you have to seek out those who are willing to establish your credit account with them. It's not especially hard to do, but it is time consuming, and we are going to show you how to do it from start-to-finish in this book. The biggest mistake you can make though, is believing that you can buy any book, anywhere, and almost instantly start getting loans and other business credit. That's not a realistic outlook, and you must always remember: if it sounds too good to be true, then it probably is too good to be true.

Keep the high fees that so-called business credit building services charge in your pockets. Read this book, and follow the information that you will find posted on our website at http://www.eagle-publications.com. Take your time, and do things properly, and you will soon be on your way to a strong credit profile.

## DEFINITIONS

- **NET 30** – A credit account that must be paid in full within 30 days
- **REVOLVING CREDIT** – A credit account that allows you to make payments based on the balance of the credit.
- **PG** – Personal Guarantee. When applying for business credit, some applications will require that you give your personal guarantee that the account will be paid under the terms of the contract.
- **USPTO** – United States Patent and Trademark Office registers patents, trademarks and service marks.

# TRADE NAMES, TRADEMARKS AND SERVICE MARKS

A trade name, obviously, is the name of your business. It's what your customers know you by when they are looking for products or services like those that you offer. Trademarks and service marks are the logos or other images that you use in conjunction with your trade name

A trademark, simply put, is associated with goods that are sold, while the service mark is associated with services that are sold. It is common to associate the term "trademark" with both products and services, and the USPTO as well as all 50 Secretary of State offices use the term interchangeably as well. In its definition, the USPTO says in its definition that a service mark is the same as a trademark except that it identifies and distinguishes the source of a service while the trademark identifies the source of goods. To be more detailed about the two terms however, Let's look at them this way:

### Trademark:

**The USPTO's definition of a trademark**: "protect words, names, symbols, sounds, or colors that distinguish goods and services from those manufactured or sold by others and to indicate the source of the goods."If your name and/or logo appears on the tangible goods that you're selling, you'd be filing for a trademark.

For instance, let's say you want to protect the name of your clothing line. As long as the name appears on the hang tag, label or the packaging that the clothes come in, that would suffice as proof of you using the name in connection with a clothing line. And therefore, you'd file for a trademark.

If the name appears only on the front of the shirt, that's ornamental use and therefore not eligible for trademark protection.

**Service Mark:**

**The USPTO's definition service mark:** "a word, name, symbol or device that is to indicate the source of the services and to distinguish them from the services of others."

If you're selling services in connection with a name and/or logo, you'd be filing for a service mark.

For example, you are opening a restaurant using a specific name. The name as it appears on any signage, menus, advertising, etc., would suffice as proof of your use in connection with your services.

Good examples of trademarks would be the font that Coca Cola uses to spell it's name, or the red, white and blue ball that Pepsi uses. A good example of a service mark is the logo that the Better Business Bureau uses. The idea behind the use of trademarks and service marks, is that when people see these logos, they will automatically think of your business. It's a long process to gain this kind of recognition. It takes many years and lots of marketing dollars to make these images do what they were intended to do, and that is to spark recognition in the minds of those who see them. That's why, in the United States at least, these marks are protected by the US government for the people that own them.

The protection afforded by the government to holders of these marks goes a little deeper that just copying the marks however. If you use a mark that is remarkably similar to a mark that is registered by another business, the government will not allow you to register it, and in some cases, you may be held liable if the holder of the original mark can prove that you caused them harm by using such a mark. The best thing that you can do when and if you decide to use a trademark or service mark, is to ensure that it is not similar to any other registered mark that is in use.

Even if the company has gone out of business, if their mark is still on file at the US Patent and Trademark Office, you can be barred from using it, because it is considered intellectual property. If you feel that you absolutely have to have that mark, and the company owning it has gone out of business, you can contact the holder, and see if they will sell it to you. A good example would be Montgomery Wards. When Wards went out of business, they had more than 100 years of providing products to people, starting out as a mail order business, eventually growing to department stores all across the United States. In 2004, a company called Direct Marketing Services, Inc saw that there was still potential in the Wards name. They then purchased the intellectual property rights for Wards which included the trademark, logos, etc. They then built a website and revived Wards as a place that people could shop, but this time online and through catalogs, effectively taking the Wards and Montgomery Ward's name back to its roots, making them a mail order house once again. There are many other examples as well, but you get the picture – if there is a trademark you want to use, do a search. If the registration has lapsed, you can register it for use yourself. If it is still active, you can look into purchasing the rights from the current trademark holder.

If you decide to make use of a trademark in your business, the best thing that you can do is to make sure that you register it. If someone else decides that they want to use it, and you do not register it, they can use it freely. If they decide to take the step of registering it, they can and they can effectively force you to STOP using it, regardless of whether you were using it first. In fact, there is a company that went to all the trouble of hiring a graphic designer and commissioned them to create a trademark for their brand. This company used this trademark for more than 10 years, but they failed to register it with the USPTO. Another company liked this logo so well, that they did a search on it and found that the first company never bothered to register it. The second company DID register it, and then started legal proceedings to force the first company to stop using the trademark. The first company went into court and showed that they had in fact commissioned the creation of the trademark, however, they lost the case because they failed to register the mark with the USPTO. If you go to the trouble of having a trademark created, make sure that you register the mark! The same thing can be said of your business name. If you are going to follow the route of setting your business up as a sole proprietorship, be sure to file a fictional name statement with the Secretary of State in the state in which you are going to conduct business. Otherwise, filing your articles of incorporation will protect you for your state.

## WHAT IS BUSINESS CREDIT?

To put it simply, business credit is similar to that of personal credit. Just like with personal credit reporting agencies, there are agencies that report on business credit. Potential creditors for your business will contact these agencies for reports on your company to assist them in making a determination as to whether they should grant your company credit. Having strong business credit is essential if your company hopes to secure a business loan at some point during its lifetime.

It's important that you establish business credit early in the life of your business so that you can separate your personal credit file from your business credit file. When your business is brand new, it is often difficult to keep the two separate. This is because your business does not yet have a credit history, and in many cases, the potential creditor will want your personal guarantee that the company bills will be paid by you, even if the company is lacking in income. The reality is, that you should ALWAYS try to keep both separated as much as possible. In fact, if you already have bad credit, and you are trying to establish business credit, it's important that you keep them separated from the beginning, or you will find that establishing business credit is even more difficult. That's the purpose of this book, to show you ways that you can establish business credit without involving your personal credit history. Don't be mistaken however – if you have bad credit on the personal side, this book is NOT going to show you how to get business loans quickly. The thought of doing so is simply not realistic. Instead, the purpose of the book is to show you how to slowly and methodically build credit while building your business into one that is financially strong and successful.

Even if you have good credit on the personal side, it's important that you work to quickly sever the credit umbilical cord between the business and your personal life. Things can and will happen in life, and if you are depending solely on your personal credit to get the business through the tough times, and something happens to mess your credit up, then you've automatically messed up your business credit too, even if the event had nothing to do with the business. Likewise, if something happens on the business side of things, it can damage your good personal credit history. Separate the two as soon as you possibly can, and then one will have no effect on the other.

When it comes to business credit, of all the credit accounts you can get, get cash loans is the most difficult. Even with established businesses, this can be difficult. It's important that you establish a good relationship with a local bank. Do all of your banking with them where possible, and make sure there are no issues with the accounts, such as overdrafts. Make it a point to get the people working within the bank, including bank officers. This is true even if y6ou do not need a cash loan right now. The relationships you build today will go a long way to helping you when the day comes that you will need help from them!

When you are running a business, regardless of size, work on building your credit. A company with a strong credit file, regardless of how small the company might be, shows that you company is legitimate. People, particularly lenders, will realize that despite the fact that you are a small operation, you are the real deal. If you have intentions of working with larger companies, or even the government, they are going to look at credit reports. A strong credit file makes it easier for your company to work with partners that are more demanding.

By establishing a business credit file, you are also working to protect personal assets from creditors if something goes wrong within your business.

Generally speaking, the greater the divide between personal and business credit, the better off you will be. In fact, if you are not careful, the courts can decide to ignore the corporate shield created when you incorporate your business.

The process that you would go through to build business credit is much the same that you would follow for building personal credit. Basically, you establish an account, pay the bills per the terms of the agreement, and over time your credit score will improve. You can also work with the credit reporting agencies to supply information that may be missing from your credit profile. The more information that is available to the reporting agency, the more your business credibility will increase. For example, submitting documents like your EIN letter from the IRS provides more information for potential creditors to look at when making decisions about extending credit to you.

As you will learn later on in this book, not all companies will report your business credit history to the reporting agencies. It's important that you try to get them to do just that so that your credit file gets stronger. Information that is not being reported does you no good. While you are working to build your credit with the vendors who extend credit to you, you can also work to build business credit by acting like a legitimate business, regardless of the size of your company. If you have a small company, and treat it as if it were your hobby, everyone else will too. Always make sure that you are following federal and state regulations for conducting business, additionally, when you apply for business credit with any company, do so under a federal EIN and not your personal social security number.

You can also incorporate your business to minimize personal liability. Incorporating used to require a lawyer, but the terms are simplified these days, and most people can incorporate a company themselves. Essentially, a corporation is doblue-taxed, meaning that the corporation pays income tax, and then any income you take from it pays income tax too, however, with the "S" corporation, the earning flow through the company and directly to you. Your tax advisor can tell you more about this, and you can also download books from the IRS website free of charge. You can find more information about the IRS forms in the resources section of this book.

Another thing to consider when is establishing business credit, specifically trying to get cash loans, is what you will use for collateral. As a new business, it is almost impossible to get a cash loan without it, and it's already hard to get a loan to begin with. Consider what you are going to use the loan proceeds for. Is it to buy equipment? If so, instead of a cash loan, why not consider leasing the equipment, with a $1.00 buyout at the end of the lease term? If you plan on buying new equipment after the initial lease-term is up, then go for the Fair Market Value type lease when the term is up. This way, the leased equipment goes back to the leasing company, and you order new equipment. It all depends on your type of business and the equipment you are leasing.

## WHY DO YOU NEED BUSINESS CREDIT?

Short and to the point: to protect your personal assets. Why would you put your personal credit and assets at risk when you don't have to? Incorporation laws, and federal tax ID numbers are there for a reason. If you don't use them to your advantage, then you risk everything that you have worked your whole life for.

Consider companies like Microsoft, Staples or any other business for that matter. Do you think they rely on their own funds for growth? NO! Even if your company is in a position of having plenty of sales and a pile of money in the bank, **THERE WILL** come a day when you will need that cash to get you through one of the many unexpected things that pop up when you least expect it. Maybe it's the loss of one of your key suppliers or a particularly talented employee. Companies that are able to beat the odds and get through the tough times are the ones that will have the best access to cash loans. When times like this arise, you will be in a position to access these loans without having to use your reserves because you had the planning and forethought to establish a strong business credit file.

Unfortunately, there are many business owners out there who have to learn things the hard way. One of the things that they learn is that trying to build a strong credit file should not begin on the day that you actually need access to the credit. According to George Ross, one of Donald Trump's attorneys, the time that you need to go to the banks for cash is BEFORE you actually need it. Likewise, the time to start building your company's credit file is from the very day you start your business. It's important that you understand that this is not just an opinion. Why do you think so many businesses fail? The first reason is lack of funding, but the second reason is lack of funds to get them through the hard times. EVERY BUSINESS SUFFERS HARD TIMES! You make a huge mistake when you believe the opposite of that statement. If you missed beginning to establish a credit file when you started your business, then do it now. Today. This is critically important to small businesses.

The Small Business Administration is very clear on just how important it is that small businesses establish a credit file. If you are already in business, you should be prepared to submit a business credit report for your company. They expect that you will be able to do this when you approach them for assistance.

For new businesses, a great way to begin building your credit report, is to establish trade lines (lines of credit) from companies that extend credit. A small business credit score is essential to separating business from personal credit. As a small business owner who is forward thinking, you will know that credit affects your ability to gain the necessary capital to get you through large orders, or to grow your company to the next level. When the time comes, and your company needs a cash infusion, you business credit file can influence the amount of a loan the bank will give you, the cost of insurance premiums that you business pays and the credit terms vendors will extend to your business.

Less than 10% of all entrepreneurs know about or understand how business credit is established and tracked. Many people believe that there is absolutely no problem with using personal credit cards, home equity or personal guarantees for business. It certainly does make getting the business started easier, but it puts your personal assets at risk if contracts are canceled, customers pay late, etc.

When you apply for a loan from a bank, the first thing they are going to check is your credit history. They will then go on to take a look at your character, company cash flow, and of course, the ability of your company to repay the loan. Collateral will of course help, but that credit report is going to go a long way toward whether the loan is approved.

Now that you have an idea on just how important business credit is, let's get a little more specific on how it works and how to establish it with this overview (we'll go into more detail later in the book).

Many people ask just how long it takes to properly build business credit. Most people automatically think of bank lines of credit when talking about business creditor, but there are also vendor lines of credit as well. Generally speaking, establishing a bank line of credit is next to impossible without first building vendor lines of credit. In this case, and in the beginning stages of your business, the vendor lines of credit are the most important at this point, because they are going to dictate what happens with the future of your company's credit.

Building a strong credit history for your company can take as many as 2-4 years and have the accounts reporting on Dun & Bradstreet, Corporate Experian and Corporate Equifax. That's why it is important that you start sooner rather than later. That is, if you work with vendors that will actually report your good payment history to the bureaus. Many people do not realize that more than 50,000 businesses will grant open accounts to their clientele. Of those 50,000, less than 10% of them even bother to report to the credit bureaus. It's because of this, that even if you do pay on time, your credit score will tend to be very low, or even non-existent. You must be sure to stay on top of things, and monitor your credit report yourself, encouraging vendors to report a good payment history when they are not. Otherwise, your hard work of building your credit profile is for nothing, because nothing is showing up.

What are the consequences if I make a mistake? Building a business credit profile is not like your personal credit profiles. With personal credit, if there is an error on your report, you can submit a letter and the personal credit bureaus are required to include it in your credit history. The law mandates this. They must also abide by certain standards of fairness and responsiveness when it comes to your personal credit history. No such rules apply when it comes to business credit. The business credit system is far less forgiving and much more difficult to navigate than the personal system. There's no entity overseeing the process and how the bureaus operate. For all intents and purposes, you have one chance at building a business credit profile correctly. Any mistakes could result in a red flag for your business for life. Once your name is associated with a business credit file, it's associated with business for life and even starting a new business may not take you away from it. Handle your business credit profile with care, because in most cases, there are no second chances.

Is this something that I can put off until later? As you might already realize from the first part of this chapter, putting off building your business credit profile until later is a risky endeavor. Business credit building requires that the process be started quickly and accurately. This book attempts to guide you in the proper direction. The rest is entirely up to you. There is no cookie cutter approach to building a strong credit profile for your business. Every individual case is unique, and it also depends on the type of business you are starting, but the reality is that the sooner you begin, the better off you and your company will be.

Now, it's already been mentioned that at one time or another, a business will suffer cash flow problems. When cash flow is troublesome, it means bills don't get paid, and employees, including YOU, do not get paid. The point being, is that you CANNOT ACCURATELY determine when cash flow will be critical. Predictions based on the history of your company can of course, help, but you cannot solely rely on those predictions.

Naturally, the best thing a company can do is set aside funds that are strictly for these rainy days, but if you have an extended period where money is tight, that savings is going to run out. Having a line of credit with your local bank can help your company survive such a crunch, but in order to establish that line of credit, you must establish a credit file so that the banks can judge whether or not you are a good credit risk. Hence, the importance of this book in getting you started in the proper direction. While your company is saving this money, it puts you in a good position of establishing the line of credit

Three good reasons to begin establishing your business credit NOW:

1. **You need access to cash**. Establishing a line of credit now, and having a good business credit report will make it easier when you approach the banks for money to continue operations. By establishing everything now, you avoid being turned down when there is a cash crunch. For instance, if the bank sees that you pay your bills on time, and you have cash in reserves, they are more likely to setup a line of credit for you than they will if you approach them with nothing. Take care that you do not use the line of credit when your company is having a serious financial crisis. These lines of credit are intended as safety nets when there are short term cash flow issues.
2. **You want to avoid the hefty fees associated with credit cards**. Credit cards can indeed help your company through a cash flow crisis. The problem is that you end up paying high rates of interest which can cause further cash flow problems. A business line of credit works much like the credit cards do, but there are lower interest rates associated with them, meaning you pay far less for the use of the money with a business line of credit than you would using credit cards.
3. **Peace of mind**. In order to apply for a line of credit, you do not have to consider cash flow problems. Think of it more as an insurance policy that will protect your business when cash flow or other issues arise that you may not have anticipated. You will be able to rest assured that if unexpected shortages at the end of the month, you'll be able to get through with you lines of credit until the cash is once again available to you.

These are all good reasons for establishing credit with a local bank, but when it comes to investing in capital improvements, or buying new equipment or fixtures, you should look into obtaining lower rate financing for those things.

# WHEN SHOULD YOU BUILD BUSINESS CREDIT?

The short answer to the question in the title is NOW. It cannot be said enough: You absolutely must separate your personal credit from your business lines. It all boils down to protecting your personal assets in case something goes wrong. According to the Small Business Administration, more than 400,000 business are started each year. Of those 400,000, 80,000 will fail rather quickly.

The primary problem for these businesses are lack of operating funds. You can avoid this by building a relationship with your local bank while your company is still flush with cash. Helping you to establish a relationship with the bank, will be the credit lines that you establish with suppliers. The suppliers will provide you with lines of credit long before a bank will. They can help however, when your D&B file, or one of the other credit reporting agencies show that you are making timely payments for the credit that has been extended to you.

Once you begin establishing credit for your business, you will find banks willing to finance you in your time of need. It may however, take several years to establish a strong credit history. Once you do, banks will begin to contact YOU to see if things are going well, and to inquire as to whether or not your company needs financing.

There are many ways to get cash you need for the company.

Venture capitalists will often give you financing. In return, they usually want a stake in the company and carry on sort of as silent partners. It depends on what kind of deal you establish with them.

With new businesses, the banks will often look at your personal credit rating. You want to try to avoid having to give a PG when you are obtaining financing and lines of credit with your vendors and the banks. Teaming up with companies such as Quill, or Uline will help you to establish trade lines that the bank can look at when you are looking for financing. Just pay the bills on time, and things will be fine.

If you process credit cards during the normal operation of your business, there are financing companies that will give you loans based on the credit activity going through your store. For instance, if you are processing say, $10,000 each month, you will be able to secure a loan based on those proceeds alone. Terms vary from one company to the next, so you have to research them carefully.

So, if you have decided that you are going into business, as soon as you have established yourself with the state, and incorporated, or setup your LLC, you need to start looking at establishing your credit file.

## WILL BUSINESS CREDIT HELP YOU TO SECURE A BUSINESS LOAN?

This entire book emphasizes the fact that you need to separate your personal credit from business lines. The fact of the matter is however, that a good personal credit history and a viable business plan is what will get you financing. Banks will look at your past payment history. You should still try to secure a business loan on the businesses own merits where possible.

If the bank insists that you start out with your personal credit history however, you should first order your credit reports from Transunion.com, Experian.com and Equifax.com. Look the reports over carefully, and attempt to eliminate anything that is negative on the report. A book entitled "*Self Help Guide to Credit Repair*" by Stephen Steinberger and published by RedStar Publications. For those reading this on tablets or Kindles, the link is clickable and will take you directly to the guide on Amazon.com.

If there is a bankruptcy on your file, it will stay there for 7 years, or longer. Banks will consider this fact and with the SBA, the bankruptcy must be more than 10-years old before they will consider you for financing.

The point, is that you must dispute everything negative on your credit report to try to have it removed. Most banks will not consider your business loan application when there is anything negative on it.

If you establish a strong credit file before applying for business loans, chances are they will not even look at your personal history.

Using a line of credit as working capital for your business helps you to easily manage cash flow. Once again, it's important that you establish this line of credit BEFORE you actually need it. Once it is established, it is as simple as writing a check that the bank provides to you that will be cashable for up to the credit limit that you have available. With the line of credit, you go to the bank once, and then establish the account. After that, you just write the check as you need the money. Payment terms are based on the deal that you establish with the entity granting you the line of credit. Make your payments as agreed, and that line of credit will quickly grow in the limits that you are permitted to use.

With a business loan, for larger investments like company growth, equipment or fixtures, and other things of that nature, the terms are different. You have to go to the bank each time you want to make a loan for these things. The loans will typically have fixed rates, and you may have to secure the loan with collateral. While the line of credit is as simple as writing the check, a larger loan will provide you with a large sum of cash, upfront, which you deposit into the company account for use in the manner that the bank approves.

Make sure that your research is thorough when you need operating cash. Sometimes you can avoid a loan altogether, and get a government grant for your company, which is provided to assist the company in succeeding. Grants do not have to be repaid. The money is essentially given to you to assist in growth, hiring employees, etc. Such grants include: Women in business, minorities in business, opening a business in an economically depressed area, etc. You obtain these grants through agencies that administer them. Simply visit www.grants.gov to see if there is a grant available for you.

The point is, whether you are looking to get a line of credit, a business loan or a grant, you must make sure that the lender only sees positive information about you and your company. Establishing your credit in the manner outlined in this book, will help you to get to the business loan point properly.

## THINGS TO AVOID WHEN BUILDING BUSINESS CREDIT

When you re trying to establish business credit, the first thing you need to avoid doing, is making payments late to creditors. Many businesses will often take as many as 90 days to pay their bills. While this is common, you should avoid doing so as much as possible and make sure the bills are paid on time, every time.

Don't buy your business credit. Many people do this, but banks frown upon it. The companies that help you to do this, are cheating the system, and credit reporting agencies will catch on to it, and they will flag your file!

The next thing that people do is to buy shelf corporations. A shelf corporation is a business that is established, and then left to sit and age. This is not a problem in and of itself, but some of the companies that sell these shelf corporations will guarantee that you will get a loan, and this is simply not true. While the lenders will in fact consider the length of time the "business" has been around, more often than not, they will know that the company has simply been left to age. Still, there are merits to buying an aged company when it comes to the creditors who will establish credit for you based on the fact that a company has been in existence for a length of time, and it does not have anything negative against it. If you decide to do something this way, you have to tread carefully, or your credit file will be flagged!

You have to make sure that establishing business credit is NOT because your personal credit is bad. Buying the book by Stephen Steinberger will help you to repair your personal credit, sometimes in as little as a year, bringing your personal credit score up. The point is to establish business credit for your company, without having it flagged because you are using the credit for personal reasons.

You also need to try to avoid securing business credit as a sole proprietor. This will tie everything to your personal credit history. If you manage your business credit poorly, it can ruin your hard work of establishing a strong business credit history, and there is no means of having things removed from a business credit file. The decisions lie sole with the credit reporting agencies as to whether or not they will remove something from your file.

The main reporting agency when it comes to business credit is Dun and Bradstreet. They provide you with the means of monitoring your business credit. Establishing a relationship with your file manager at D&B can help to make sure that you credit file stays clean. There are other agencies as well, including Experian.com and Equifax.com, that will maintain credit files for your business, but D&B is the one that is regularly used.

All you have to do, is take care and do things properly, and your business credit file will carry you and your company where it needs to go!

## WHAT ARE BUSINESS CREDIT BUREAUS?

A business credit bureau is very much like the personal credit bureaus. They report the same as well, but they are not regulated as strictly as they are for personal credit.

Experian.com and Equifax.com do have their footprint in the business credit reporting arena. Dun and Bradstreet however, strictly concentrates on the business sector, and they are the company that is used most often to determine whether or not a creditor will establish a credit line for you.

In many cases, it is you that will have to register yourself with the business credit bureaus. When you apply for business credit, the creditor will contact one of these agencies. If you have no credit, they will simply see an empty file. Banks will often turn down credit when there is nothing in the file. The smaller companies however, will often give your company a chance. They will then report your payment activity to the bureaus, and your payment history will reflect whet6her or not you get credit from some of the other companies. For instance, for office supplies, people often go to Quill.com, who will easily approve credit for you when you orders are smaller than $200.00. Uline will grant initial credit on a web order if the order is $400.00 or less. In this case, the company in question has no credit history, so there is nothing negative to stop them from granting you credit. You then grow from there adding the harder companies as your business grows.

So, basically, a business credit bureau is an agency that will dictate whether or not a company or a bank will grant credit to you. It's really not that hard to establish a good credit history. You just have to give it time to grow, and always make sure that payments are made in a timely manner.

# HOW TO SETUP A NEW BUSINESS

The first thing that you need to do when you start a business is to consider the type of business you are going to form. Frankly, starting as a sole proprietor will lock you into gaining credit on a personal level in most cases. LLC's can now operate much like a corporation. With a corporation, you can choose to form your company as a class C corporation, or an S corporation With an S corporation, the funds flow through the company to you. With a class C, you pay income tax on the business income, and then income tax on what you take as personal earnings. This guide is not going to detail the exact steps to forming a company, but it will give you the basis. These steps are:

1. Register with the IRS and get an EIN. If you operate as a sole proprietor, you will not need an EIN. You simply use your social security number, unless you are going to hire employees.
2. Register your company with the state. If you are going to operate as a sole proprietor, you must file a fictional name statement. Some states may call it a business name registration. If you are going to operate as an LLC or a corporation, you must file papers with the state as appropriate. You must visit your state's Secretary of State page to learn the rules for your area.
3. Establish your business bank account. A business bank account will help to keep personal and business finances separate.
4. Use the information you now have about your company to

begin establishing credit with the various vendors that you need to deal with.

You will also need to develop a strong business plan. Creditors like banks will want to see this. You can get business plan software relative cheap from Amazon. The best software available seems to be Business Plan Pro. The link is clickable in the ebooks. For those reading the paperback version of the book, go to http://amzn.to/17L6RlA and you will get a good deal. At the time of publication, the software is only $34.99 and it offers sample plans to give you a starting point. Fill in the blanks, and the software will do the rest.

When you are just starting out, you are going to need some sort of funding. More often than not, business operators will contribute their own money for the startup. Other funds can be gotten from family members. It's going to be difficult in the outset to start a business as far as operating cash goes. Many people will use the equity in their homes. If you have to do this, make sure you work hard at separating what you do with the business from your personal credit. The startup funds can be considered loans, and then paid back when the cash starts to flow. Even money that you contribute yourself can be repaid and written off on the tax returns.

If your business is in a physical location, where people will be coming and going, you will need to get liability insurance in case something happens and you get sued.

Finally, you need to establish some sort of an accounting system. The most popular software seems to be Quickbooks. Using that is easy and you can have your company ledgers set up quickly. For those using the paperback version of this book, the link is http://amzn.to/181F8dt This is Quickbooks Simple Start, and it has the lower pricing for startup. You can upgrade to the more sophisticated version of the program later on, when the company starts to grow.

The book "Business Startup Guide", by Eagle Publications, due out December 12, 2013 will go into more detail on actually establishing your company.

# ASSET PROTECTION

One of the most important things that you need to do when you start your company, is to protect your personal assets in case of business failure. This chapter will be short and to the point. PROTECT YOUR PERSONAL ASSETS! Forming your business as an LLC or a corporation will help you to do this. Each state has different rules, so you need to research these rules with them, and the Internal Revenue service before you actually establish the company. Read about the best way to protect personal assets from those of your company.

You can also protect assets by establishing certain retirement funds. If the business fails, and creditors start coming after you for money, if you do not properly protect these assets, they can be taken to repay debt. You ABSOLUTELY MUST secure and maintain an account who will be able to protect things for you. Protecting assets is not like hiding them, it just establishes funds that can not be taken from you.

# ABOUT BUSINESS STRUCTURES

Once again, this guide is not a detailed book on establishing your new company. The business startup guide that we will soon publish is intended to help you do that. Still, we will talk a little about the different business structures here.

The most basic type of business is the sole proprietorship. With this type of business. You alone own the company and its assets. These basically become personal assets, leaving your personal stuff wide open if the business fails.

The next form of business is the Limited Liability Company, or an LLC. This type of company is intended to provide the features of limited liability of a corporation while leaving the flexible operation and tax efficiencies available from the Internal Revenue Service. Research the rules for your state before you actually establish your company as an LLC.

Next is the corporation. Corporations are setup as a C corporation or an S corporation. For taxing purposes, the S corporation allows funds to flow through the business and the profits become the income for the operator(s) of the company. You then report the taxes on your form 1040, although the company still has to file an 1120S form each year.

Next is the partnership. You establish this partnership by filing a partnership agreement. The partners then become responsible for the assets and liabilities of the company, at a percentage that depends on the number of partners. For instance, if there are two partners, each has a 50% stake in the company. Likewise, if there are five partners, then each is responsible for 20%.

## COMPANIES THAT OFFER NET 30 TERMS

There Are MANY companies out there that will offer you net 30 terms. This means that they will ship product to you, and you will pay the invoices within 30 days of the order. Most of these companies report your payment history to D&B, but some will not. If you establish net 30 terms with a company, encourage them to report your payment history. This establishes trade lines on your credit report that other companies will look at and make a decision as to whether or not to establish a credit account for you. If a company turns you down for credit, reapply to them in a couple of months. This just means that you don't yet have enough history for them to decide as to whether they will open an account for you. The phone numbers provided are contact number that you must call to get their application faxed or emailed to you. Keep in mind that things change often, and you might have to go to their website to get the updated number. Some applications can be downloaded on our website at www.eagle-publications.com. Go to the members area and register. You will then have access to the forms.

1. **Quill Office Products**: www.quill.com
2. **Uline**: offers shipping and other supplies to companies. They also have some furniture and other things like that which you might need. www.uline.com
3. **Arco:** Fuel cards for businesses www.arco.com 800-348-7959
4. **Branders**: This company offers promotional products

designed to advertise your company. www.branders.com
5. **CompUSA Commercial** offers office supplies and equipment. Fill out the online application to establish an account at www.compusa.com
6. **Deluxe Checks**: Business and personal check printers., 1-800-328-8473
7. **Fedex-Kinkos**: Offers printing, packaging and shipping. www.fedex.com
8. **Gemplers**: Outdoor work supplies, boots, personal protection equipment, etc. www.gemplers.com
9. **Graingers**: offers outdoor supplies, MRO supplies and equipment. 1-888-361-8569 www.grainger.com
10. **Home Depot Commercial**: building supplies and tools. www.homedepot.com 1-888-875-5489 ext. 1
11. **Interstate**: mainly supplies batteries of al types. 1-856-241-1188 eee.interstate.com
12. **Rapid Forms**: offers all sorts of form printed and customized for your company. 1-800-257-5287 www.rapidforms.com
13. **Reliable**: offers office supplies and equipment. This company seems to be choosy, so you may have to pay cash in the beginning to establish an account with them. www.reliable.com 1-800-359-5000
14. **Sam's Club Commercial**: offers all sorts of things including office supplies and equipment, store stock, tires, etc. www.samsclub.com 800-203-5764
15. **Seton**: offers signage, labels, etc. 1-800-571-2596 www.seton.com
16. **Shell Commercial**: Fuel cards www.shell.com 1-888-335-8423
17. **Staples Business**: offers office supplies and equipment. www.staples.com 1-800-282-5316
18. **Tech Depot**: Supplies and primarily business equipment. Owned by Office Depot. This company seems to be easier to get credit from than going to Office Depot. Sometimes you can simply place an order on their site and request that it be an open account. They will check your DUNS file for your credit history. It can take a few days to hear back from them. www.techdepot.com 1-800-625-9866

19. **Texaco Commercial**: Fuel cards www.texaco.com 1-888-716-0018
20. **Uline**: Sometimes, simply placing an order online will establish an open account for you. They will check your DUNS file usually. www.uline.com 1-800-295-5510
21. **UPS**: Shipping services. www.ups.com 1-800-742-5727
22. **JC Penney Commercial**: domestic items, clothing, bedding, furniture, etc. www.jcpenney.com 1-800-527-4403
23. **Mobil Gas**: Fuel cards www.mobil.com 1-800-950-6095
24. **Walmart Commercial**: Purchase from Walmart on net 30 terms. www.walmart.com 1-877-294-7548
25. **Wearmark**: Actually Aramark. They offer uniforms and clothing. www.shoparamark.com 1-800-388-3300
26. **Nebs**: Offers forms, checks, etc. www.nebs.com 1-888-823-6327
27. **Office Depot**: Offers office supplies and equipment. www.officedepot.com 1-800-767-1358
28. **PC Mall**: Computers and other office equipment. www.pcm.com 1-800-504-8218
29. **Radio Shack Commercial**: Buy from Radio Shack on net 30 terms. 1-800-442-7221
30. **Demco**: Furniture and equipment www.demco.com 1-800-356-1200

There are literally thousands of more companies willing to extend you credit to help out with your business. Just remember to remind them to report your good payment history to D&B at the very least!

## COMPANIES THAT OFFER REVOLVING ACCOUNTS

There are a number of companies that offer revolving credit accounts. It works much like a credit card for the store. You make your purchases, and then pay the minimum monthly payment. You can purchase up to your established credit limit. The credit limit will grow as you make payments to them on time. Likely every 3-6 months. If they don't automatically increase you limit, give them a call and it is very likely that that they will increase it while you are on the phone with them!

1. **Walmart**: offers business revolving credit to buy the merchandise that they sell. You will have a fixed credit limit, and you simply make payments as per the agreement. www.walmart.com
2. **Sam's Club**: Same as Walmart. You must be a member of the club to get the benefits of purchasing. www.samsclub.com
3. **Dell Computers**: Computer supplies and equipment. Apply to this one after you have established a credit profile. www.dell.com
4. **Amazon**: Offers business credit to purchase virtually anything that they sell. www.amazon.com
5. **US Bank Skypass Visa**: They will check your personal credit history despite the many claims that they do not. www.usbank.com

6. **Target**: Same as Walmart. www.target.com

Gas cards are also available to businesses. They are intended really to maintain control and to help you stay on top of fuel costs for your company. Most will check personal credit, unless your business is at least 3 years old.

1. **Conoco/76**: www.conoco.com
2. **Shell Gasoline**: www.shell.com
3. **Exxon/Mobil**: www.exxon.com
4. **Chevron**: www.chevron.com
5. **Sunoco**: www.sunoco.com

A revised list of both companies that offer revolving accounts and net 30 terms will be added to the members section of our website as they become known to us.

## OTHER RESOURCES

Many resources were used in the creation of this guide. Some of the information included here was found on these websites. Please visit and support these companies where possible, because they are the ones that make your business life easier as you learn and grow your company!

1. www.Mashable.com
2. www.Entrepreneur.com
3. www.sba.gov
4. www.foxbusiness.com
5. www.experian.com
6. www.dnb.com
7. www.creditcards.com
8. www.wellsfargo.com
9. www.eagle-publications.com

People that join our members section on our website get all sorts of benefits, including access to download updates to our guides, free webhosting, discounted domain names and much more. They also get books and guides that are discounted to as much as 50% off or more! Go to www.eagle-publications.com/members Our forum will also be available for you to ask questions and get answers when starting your business!

# BUILDING CREDIT FOR YOUR BUSINESS

# ABOUT EAGLE PUBLICATIONS

Eagle Publications was formed in May 2013 as a publishing company. When creator John Derossett realized that he needed to separate the two types of books being published by the company, he formed RedStar Publications to publish the mainstream books the company was producing, and to serve as the parent company for the publishing group he was building.

Eagle Publications then began serving as the branch publishing business oriented books such as Building Credit for Your Business and the Business Startup Guide. To this end, we have embarked on building a website intended to serve startup businesses, including everything from providing the material explaining how to get started, all the way down to hosting your business related website.

The goal of Eagle Publications is to help people start a new business, and help it to survive when times get rough.

www.ingramcontent.com/pod-product-compliance
Lightning Source LLC
Chambersburg PA
CBHW051823170526
45167CB00005B/2140